How to Get 50+ BOOMER FITNESS CLIENTS FAST

How to Get 50+
BOOMER
FITNESS
CLIENTS
FAST

Dan Ritchie, PhD and Cody Sipe, PhD

Co-Founders, Functional Aging Institute

©2018; revised 2019, 2021
Published by Niche Pressworks
for Functional Aging Institute

Functional Aging Institute – **FunctionalAgingInstitute.com**

Niche Pressworks – **NichePressworks.com**

Contents

What Works for Us

Dan Ritchie and I (Cody Sipe) met in college at Purdue University in West Lafayette, Indiana. At the time, I was wrapping up my PhD studies in Kinesiology, and he was just beginning his PhD. (Dan also has a minor in Gerontology—the study of aging.)

Both of us were fascinated by the study of health and fitness in people over age 65, so we spent several years researching and then actually experimenting on this demographic.

We got permission from Purdue University to take people over age 65 through power training, balance training, obstacle courses, and all kinds of innovative stuff.

Contrary to popular belief about older adults at the time, nobody died from taking on more involved fitness training.

In fact, we saw some amazing outcomes.

We saw that some people can get more powerful at an older age. People can improve their balance, decrease their falls, and move better. And, we documented that if the exercise program is innovative and well thought out, older adults get great results, just like younger adults.

The more we learned, the more excited we got about what was possible for this underserved market of people in their 60s, 70s, 80s, and beyond.

Their focus was different. It wasn't about looking great in a bikini, or getting six-pack abs. They were interested in functional fitness—learning techniques

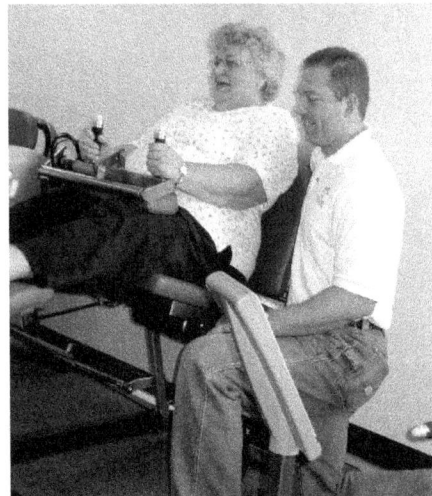

that would allow them to continue doing the things they loved to do, wanted to do, and had to do to stay healthy and active.

They want to continue to do things like golf, tennis, hiking, biking, dancing at their grandchild's wedding, going on exotic vacations, taking care of their home, gardening, etc. And, most important to many, they want to maintain their independence and avoid moving to an assisted living community or nursing home.

So, we worked on developing our initial ideas to maximize the functional ability of older adults—things that were contrary to the common practice of repetitive machine sets and cardio.

Along the way, we were mentored by and collaborated with some of the top researchers, pioneers, and experts in exercise for older adults. These include Debra Rose, Wojtek Chodzko-Zajko, Roseann Lyle, Jessie Jones, and Roberta Rikli, to name a few. Those relationships and our connection with America College of Sports Medicine (ACSM) helped shape what is now the Functional Aging Training model.

Since there were very few studios in the US that focused on the older adult, we decided to launch our own. Miracles Fitness in West Lafayette, Indiana, became a proving ground for our functional fitness ideas and strategies.

After several years of remarkable success, we found we wanted to make a much greater impact and share our success globally—and that's how the Functional Aging Institute (FAI) began.

Now, Dan and I speak on functional fitness for older adults at almost every major fitness conference, and FAI has courses and certifications teaching these skills to personal trainers around the world.

Our goal is to positively impact more than 10 million lives through the Functional Aging Institute by helping thousands of trainers like you profitably attract and train the mature adult population.

We are already well on our way to 10,000 trainers who, in turn, should each impact 1000 client lives over their career.

In this book, we're going to show you the techniques that work for us and our certified trainers to help make that impact.

These ideas have been proven successful in all types of communities—from big cities where competing fitness centers are literally next door to one another, to rural communities with populations so low their profits defy expectations.

Let's get moving.

Please note: Throughout this book, we share some of our business success stories and the success stories of our clients and members. There are no typical results, and your results may vary based on any number of factors. As with all things, building a strong profitable business that you enjoy takes consistent effort and self-discipline. Just like staying fit for life.

Chapter 1

Why There's a TON of Money in Boomer Fitness

One of the questions we often get from trainers is, "Can you really build a business and be successful in the fitness industry by focusing on older adults?"

There are a lot of misconceptions about who really are the prime fitness clientele.

For decades, we've been told that the prime clientele is somewhere in their 20s or 30s—they want six-pack abs, they want big guns, and they want to fit into their skinny jeans.

Well, that used to be the prime clientele, but you know what? Most trainers never made a successful living with that so-called "prime" clientele.

Think about how many times have you considered quitting the industry, and how many solid trainers you have seen come and go over the years.

The reality is that the prime clientele you can really build a viable business opportunity around is much older.

The prime clientele is in their 50s, 60s, and even 70s. These are the aging Boomers, what we call the mature market.

This is really a perfect storm that is brewing in the fitness industry; one you should be positioned to take advantage of.

It's an opportunity that could propel your business to the next level and set it on a course of success for the next 20, 30, or 40 years.

There are nearly 75 million Boomers right now—adults between the ages of 54 and 72 years old.[1]

These are huge numbers of potential clients. But, more than that, not only are there huge numbers, they need what fitness offers them.

Because they are getting older, they are starting to feel those aches in their joints, starting to get saggy around the middle, starting to realize they are slower of step, and they understand that they really need fitness.

They want what fitness can give them and understand its benefits.

We have a population of mature adults that don't want to just live life; they want to live life fully.

They don't want to "grow old and weak" like their parents did.

They don't want to sit in rocking chairs and watch the world go by.

They want to continue to work if they want, to contribute to society, to volunteer, to travel, and to spend time with their kids and grandkids.

They want to do all these things, which is why they understand and want what fitness can give them.

AND they have the money to pay for it.

This is a very wealthy market. They have way more disposable income than the younger adult market does. They have more net worth and control about 80% of our nation's discretionary spending.

They are inclined to spend money on the things they value.

They value fitness, so you are in a position to take advantage of what we call the Longevity Economy.

---

[1] Fry, Richard. "Millennials overtake Baby Boomers as America's largest generation." Fact Tank. April 25, 2016. Accessed February 20, 2018. http://www.pewresearch.org/fact-tank/2016/04/25/millennials-overtake-baby-boomers/.

The Longevity Economy

The Longevity Economy is every aspect of the economy associated with the 50+ market—all the goods and services that they purchase to serve their needs.

The wealth of adults over 50 in the US alone is larger than the economy of any other country except the US and China. That is, only the US and China have national economies larger than the combined spending power of mature adults in America.[2]

It's REMARKABLE that the Longevity Economy is larger than the ENTIRE economy of Japan, UK, or Germany!

And it's going to continue growing! Check out this chart[3], and note the angle of the line where we are right now in 2018!

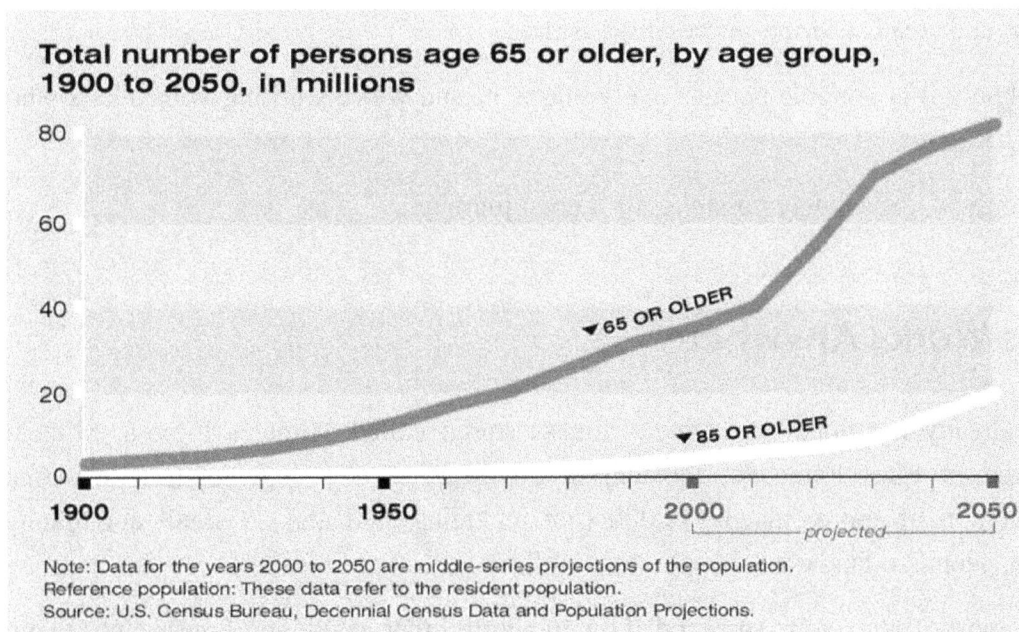

Total number of persons age 65 or older, by age group, 1900 to 2050, in millions

Note: Data for the years 2000 to 2050 are middle-series projections of the population.
Reference population: These data refer to the resident population.
Source: U.S. Census Bureau, Decennial Census Data and Population Projections.

We are talking about a rapidly growing economic force that's virtually untapped! And yet CrossFit, big-box gyms, YMCA's, personal training studios, etc., are still bending over

[2] Coughlin, Joseph F. The Longevity Economy: Inside the World's Fastest-Growing, Most Misunderstood Market. New York, NY: PublicAffairs, 2017.

[3] Bureau, US Census. "Library." An Aging World. March 28, 2016. Accessed February 22, 2018. https://www.census.gov/library/visualizations/2016/comm/cb16-54_aging_world.html.

backwards chasing younger buyers because they don't understand how to train anyone else.

At this point, you should be saying to yourself ...

> *Instead of going after the same 20- and 30-year-old market that everybody else is going after, I need to reposition myself so I can take advantage of this growing mature adult population that is going to continue growing for the next 30 to 40 years.*

This is the dominant market in our society today, and it's one that the vast majority of personal trainers and fitness professionals are missing out on.

It is not even on their radar so you have a remarkable opportunity to get in now, get in early, and create a strong, successful business.

We know it is possible because we've done it, and we're working with others who are doing it too.

Not only is it absolutely possible, it's a great journey.

This Works Anywhere

We already mentioned we have a fitness studio called Miracles Fitness. Miracles is located in West Lafayette, Indiana, in the heart of a college town with a general population of approximately 32,000 (not including students). A small community by many people's standards.

Like most of you, we're surrounded by numerous other health and fitness clubs that offer more amenities and lower membership fees—including big-box chains, popular new community centers, the YWCA and YMCA, and even Purdue University with its state-of-the-art new recreational facility for students and faculty.

Despite all that competition, our business is thriving.

Our average private training client pays $500 per month, and our group training programs average $200 per month. All of our clients are on recurring monthly billing or annual payment plans.

Our total revenue averages just about $700,000 a year. Not bad for a mid-size community with plenty of fitness options. More importantly, our retention rate averages at least three years, and it's climbing with every year we're in operation.

FAI also hosts a private mastermind for personal trainers. Our members represent a wide assortment of fitness innovators—from those in big cities with fitness centers literally on every block, to rural Canadian communities with almost no competition.

They're a mix of studio owners, franchise owners, and in-home services.

Every area has its challenges and its opportunities. The secret is knowing your market and your numbers so you can build a profitable business.

Let's do some quick math.

In this box, write the amount of NEW revenue you'd like to ADD to your business this year.

$_____

Now, calculate what your ideal client is worth to you per month. You may have two numbers:

Average Private Lesson Fee $_____ per month

Average Group Lesson Fee $_____ per month

In general, small groups are the most profitable use of your time. Each client pays less, but with 4–6 in a group, you should be earning more per hour than you can working one-on-one with clients.

A lot of Boomers prefer the small groups for the social interaction, so we recommend moving as many clients to groups as possible.

Now, multiply your average monthly membership rate x 12 months to determine what each client is worth to you on an annual basis.

Private Fee $ _____ x 12 = $ _____ = annual value of that client

Group Fee $ _____ x 12 = $ _____ = annual value of that client

Now, divide your revenue goal by one or an average of both numbers to determine how many new Boomer fitness clients you need to hit your revenue growth goal.

| $ | / | $ | = | # |

Revenue Goal   /   Average Annual Value   =   New Members

Remember that new member number. It's the target you could reach using the marketing ideas from rest of this book!

7 More Reasons You Should Train Mature Adults

1. There Are a LOT of Boomers Looking for Better Options

Mature adults don't want to work out at a gym next to 20- and 30-year-old "kids." Their values, their interests, and their motives are entirely different.

And their training goals are very different.

They want experiences that cater to them and their unique needs.

They want professional expertise. Someone they know understands their needs and won't risk hurting them.

They realize many things may be too demanding for their bodies. They don't want to be treated like they are old, but they can't risk getting injured either.

We'll talk more about branding to attract them later in the book, but, for now, just realize that they want something better than just another trainer in the closest gym.

Baby Boomers in the US are the wealthiest generation in the history of humanity, and they are about to inherit 17 trillion dollars from their traditionalist parents.[4] This is considered the largest transfer of wealth in the history of the world!

They have the money; they have built the path to retirement; and now they realize they need the physical ability, the functional ability, and the vitality to enjoy it all.

Apparently, you can have your cake and eat it too … if you have the physical ability!

2. The Aging Market Is Still Growing

Over the next 20–30 years, the mature market is poised to grow over 33%, while the 18–49 market will stay relatively stagnant at around 10-12% growth.[5]

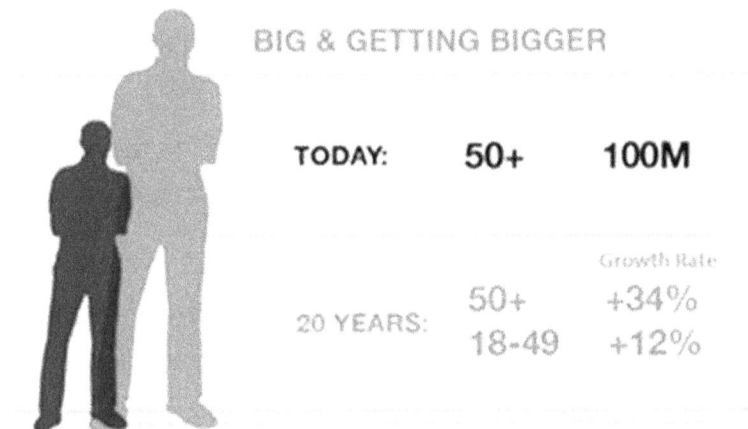

BIG & GETTING BIGGER

		Growth Rate
TODAY:	50+	100M
20 YEARS:	50+	+34%
	18-49	+12%

Get that?

If you stay with the under-49 crowd, your clients will be aging out of your market faster than they're coming in!

---

[4] Coughlin, Joseph F. The Longevity Economy: Inside the World's Fastest-Growing, Most Misunderstood Market. New York, NY: PublicAffairs, 2017.
[5] Ibid.

This is a time like we have never seen in human history! Never have so many people lived beyond 65 and for so long!

One hundred years ago, life expectancy was right around 50 years of age. Now, if you're a woman in your 60s, you have a one-in-three chance of living to 100.[6]

The 50+ and 60+ market is exploding in growth and will continue to grow through 2050.

This is not a small niche or a new specialty market segment. This is the fastest growing age group, and they just happen to a have disproportionate amount of time and spending power!

3. Boomers Have Better Schedules

One of the biggest benefits to trainers who are used to working-age adults is the older adult's schedule.

Let's face it, the typical fitness work schedule doesn't make for a great work/life balance. You're up at 4am and train clients until 10am. Then, you work out yourself, have lunch, take a nap, run some errands, and start your workday again at 4pm and train until 8pm. You get home just in time to kiss your kids good night and get to bed so you can do it all over again tomorrow.

Most trainers leave the industry in three to five years due to the real lack of stable work hours. You simply cannot sustain a work life designed around "regular" people's work hours.

Boomers solve this problem, particularly if they're retired, because they're willing and desiring to train at 8am, 9am, 10am, 11am, noon, 1pm ...

You can have normal working hours—6am to 2pm, or 7am to 3pm, or even 8am to 4pm—AND have a full schedule of clients who don't cancel on a whim because they're not giving fitness a backseat to work and parenting!

---

[6] National Center for Health Statistics, "Health, United States, 2016: With Chartbook on Long-Term Trends in Health," Life expectancy at birth, at age 65, and at age 75, by sex, race, and Hispanic Origin: United States, selected years 1900-2015 Table 15, https://www.cdc.gov/nchs/data/hus/hus16.pdf#015 (accessed February 20, 2018).

In the US, 10,000 Boomers are turning 65 (retirement age) every day and another 10,000 are turning 70 every day[7]. They are primed for the next chapter of life and available to fill up your training schedule from 9am to 4pm!

4. Boomers Are Highly Self-Motivated

There's a big difference between a client who's working out because she really wants to lose weight before her wedding versus a 70-year-old woman who is determined not to end up in a nursing home.

The mature adult and senior's workout ethic includes both urgency and a long-term focus.

They don't need constant cheerleading and reminders to show up and work on their goals. In fact, you'll find many of them are more driven to exercise than you are!

These people aren't taking retirement lying down or going quietly off into the sunset. They have dreams and hopes for years to come, and fitness is a tool for them to accomplish so much more in life!

The Baby Boomer generation was the original WIFM (What's In It For Me?) generation! They are highly driven and motivated to be the best, have the best, and work with the best services.

5. Boomers Are Happier Clients

Let's be honest for a minute. The typical younger training client often comes for one reason: they are unhappy about the way they look, or they desperately want to lose weight.

Yet, as trainers, we know that much of appearance and weight loss is tied to much more than exercise. Sleep, stress, and, of course, nutrition factor in as much as what happens while they're with us for a couple hours a week.

---

[7] USNews & World Report, "The Baby Boomer Number Game," March 23, 2012. https://money.usnews.com/money/blogs/on-retirement/2012/03/23/the-baby-boomer-number-gamehttps://www.cdc.gov/nchs/data/hus/hus16.pdf#015 (accessed February 20, 2018).

As much as we might coach them on those things, we don't live with them, cook for them, or have much ability to manage their stress.

So, after six months and only 12 pounds of weight loss they complain, get depressed, and think it is our fault as trainers that their lives are a mess.

And then, of course, there are the rock star clients that lose 40 pounds and love the results we got them … and, after a few more months, they realize they just can't "afford" to keep training. We got them where they wanted to be so they really don't "need" us anymore.

These sorts of examples rarely, if ever, happen with Boomers as clients.

First, they are much, much less focused on weight loss and appearance. Sure, they want to look good and maybe losing weight would be nice, but they are much more focused on health, movement quality, and energy.

If they do lose weight, it's a bonus that came from choosing to work with you on their long-term goal.

When you take a 62-year-old who is feeling their age to a 63-year-old who feels 50 again, they are hooked on you for years to come!

6. Boomers Are Very Loyal Clients

Speaking of loyalty … it's no surprise that the under-40 crowd tends to be a fickle buyer. They're seeing workout challenges on Instagram, YouTube, Facebook, and Pinterest, and they're easily hooked to try the newest fad.

By contrast, people over 50 aren't swayed by what's hot now. Once they find something that works for them, they stick with it.

Miracles Fitness just celebrated its 11th year in business and several of our clients have been with us from the start—some even from years before we opened!

The average Boomer at Miracles will remain a client for 4–5 years versus the industry average of 6–9 months for the under-50 crowd.

Once we get their business, we know we're probably going to keep them for another 5, 10, 15 years!

When people ask us who the best client is, we always ask them, "Would you rather train people that are broke and can't afford to stay more than six months or people that get hooked on you and need you for the rest of their lives?"

If you sign up a 57-year-old who likes surfing and skiing, he's going to be committed to staying fit because he wants to KEEP surfing and skiing. He knows you're helping him do that so you have him hooked, and he is not going anywhere.

They aren't signing your contract thinking you're a short-term fix to help them "fit into a wedding dress" or "look good for a 20th high school reunion" or "lose 20 pounds, or else."

They are signing up to be the best version of themselves for years to come. YEARS, not months. They are in this for the long haul with you if you take good care of them.

Many of our clients at Miracles Fitness have outlasted our trainers! Our trainers stay an average of three to four years. They move away, have babies, open their own training studios, etc. Many of our clients outlast them by twice that long!

7. Price Is NOT an Issue

For this audience, fitness is an investment in their rich, diverse portfolio.

A good-quality candidate will pay 3 to 5 times the normal rate if they believe what you offer is the best. You don't have to worry about the latest health club popping up for $25 or even $10 a month. It won't even catch their eye.

Now this doesn't mean they will pay exorbitant prices or be happy to overpay.

But if they value your service and you deliver results, you will not hear price objections. They will renew again and again and again, year after year.

Many will happily pay in full for $3,000 to $6,000 contracts because they are committed for at least a year—especially women, who reportedly make the decision on how to spend up to 70-80% of a household's discretionary budget. A payment plan is not something they need.

Remember! They are enjoying a stage in life where the house is paid for, the car is paid for, college for the kids is done, their kids are married with jobs, etc.

It's now THEIR TIME. They have money, and they have discretionary spending power.

Chapter 2

The Secret to Marketing to Boomers

Let's talk about how marketing to mature adults is different than marketing to people under 50.

Over the years, entertainment and advertising have been embarrassingly guilty of ageism—portraying mature adults as weak, frail, inactive, and sickly, with declining mental capabilities.

Poking fun at "old age" may have aroused chuckles in the '80s and '90s, but that audience grew up, and they're not laughing anymore.

- **71% of adults over the age of 55 feel advertising doesn't reflect their current lifestyle.**[8]

- **Two thirds of Baby Boomers admit they're so disgusted by the media disconnect that they're tuning out.** [9]

Get that? They're actually TURNED OFF by the marketing messages targeted AT THEM!

The fitness industry is one of the worst culprits. We've been devastatingly woeful at serving the 50+ market.

We post sweaty body-builder shots of people 20 years younger than them while talking about bikinis and six-pack abs. Or, we use stock art images of wrinkled, gray-haired models lifting wimpy 5 pound weights as we talk about strength training!

What a disaster!

---

[8] Global Population Ageing: Peril or Promise? Geneva: World Economic Forum, 2012.
[9] Ibid.

Not only is the imagery wrong, the entire message is wrong!

We don't want to be marketing fitness at all!

The mature market wants what fitness can give them. They don't want fitness.

We THINK they want fitness so they can get in shape and tone up their muscles.

We start thinking and talking about fitness terms because we are fitness people.

But that's not what they want.

They want health, longevity, and more life experiences … maybe with their younger family members.

Our kids' grandparents travel with us a lot. They want to go on vacation with us to Disney, the beach, hiking in Colorado, overseas, everywhere. Fortunately, we love having them with us.

Those opportunities are really what they want, NOT FITNESS. We could never sell our in-laws on fitness programming.

But, at some point, they finally realized, "If we're going to enjoy Colorado with you and go hiking, we probably better start training for this," and they did. The result was very helpful because we could go on one to five mile hikes, rather than a flat, half-mile loop that goes nowhere.

We've said it before and it bears repeating:

Boomers don't want to just spend money on things they need. They actually have the dollars and the desire to splurge on things they truly want.

That's what makes this audience so exciting!

So how do we make them really *want* our fitness programs?

Talk about what they ALREADY want.

First, you capture the desires of their heart. Then you get their minds by showing them how to achieve what they want. That's how you'll earn their business.

Got that? Speak to their heart.

Capture Their Heart Through Stories

The best marketing tool for this audience is storytelling. You capture their interest by sharing your own experiences and the experiences of others. This helps them build a belief in their own life-changing story.

1. Start by Telling YOUR Story

If you want people to know, like, and trust you, you've got to be human and relatable.

One of our FAI Mastermind clients had her business for nearly 16 years and she'd never told anyone about her struggle with addiction and how exercise helped her recover. It took a little convincing, but we urged her to write about it in a series of emails to her clients and prospects.

She did.

That's when people started emotionally connecting with her, and new business started pouring in.

Now, that series of ten emails is part of every new prospect's welcome email campaign. They're so authentic and compelling they convert like crazy!

You may not have a dramatic story, but you do have a story. Tell people why you chose fitness as a career. What inspired you then and what (and who) inspires you now.

2. Share Your Clients' Success Stories

Big successes, little achievements. Share as many and as often as you can.

A lot of trainers say they have lots of testimonials, but, are you sharing them? Are you writing them in emails? Are you posting them on Facebook? Are you putting up pictures or getting them on video?

Or, do you just have them appear somewhere … once … like on your gym wall?

You have to put them out on Facebook and talk about them often.

When a 72-year-old prospect is learning about us, and they are thinking, "I don't know if I can go hiking across Europe with my family." We can share the story of one of our clients (someone they may actually know) and say, "Well, Joanne went in her 80s … and, oh, by the way, she did it with Parkinson's."

We have to be able to put positive aging paradigms in front of them.

You have to tell these stories.

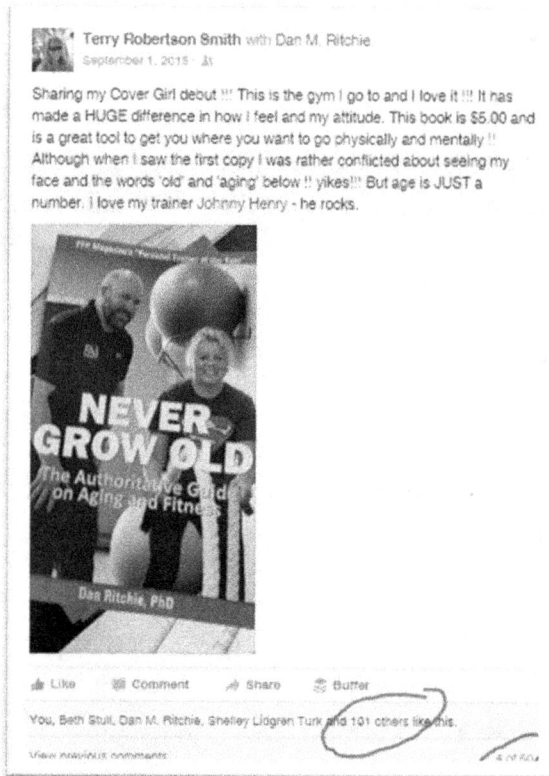

Terry Robertson Smith with Dan M. Ritchie
September 1, 2015 ·

Sharing my Cover Girl debut !!! This is the gym I go to and I love it !!! It has made a HUGE difference in how I feel and my attitude. This book is $5.00 and is a great tool to get you where you want to go physically and mentally !! Although when I saw the first copy I was rather conflicted about seeing my face and the words 'old' and 'aging' below !! yikes!!! But age is JUST a number. I love my trainer Johnny Henry - he rocks.

3. Create Stars

We create stars at Miracles through storytelling. You should do this too by making a big deal out of your biggest success stories.

Lance is one of our most popular stars. He's on the cover our first book, and he was in a lot of our original ads. We (and he) love to tell the story about the day he discovered that his workouts at Miracles used many of the same drills as the Purdue Football team—battle ropes, burpees, planks, etc. He did them all, and he was 84 years old!

Terry loved her stardom when we put her on the cover of our second book. As a former owner of a popular floral shop in town, she's extremely well known in the community. Anyone that bought or got flowers—for an anniversary, wedding, or funeral—probably got them from Terry. Making her our cover star helped us get a lot of extra mileage out of the social media attention that naturally came with her and the book.

Joyce, Joanne, Bill, etc. … we tell their stories and feature them in as many ways as possible to make them stars.

Sharing their stories makes them feel great, which reinforces their efforts, which makes them more loyal … AND it inspires others!

Just remember—you have to showcase the positive aging paradigm in your market so people take notice.

You may be the ONLY ONE in your community showcasing the positive side of aging and what it means to age well.

If storytelling is the first key to marketing to the mature market, the second one is this.

Tell Them Exactly What to Do Next

We've learned this is one thing that is a little bit different from most markets.

Most 20-, 30-, and 40-year-old adults will see your promotion and figure out really quickly, "Oh, it's a 21-day fitness plan for $67. I pay online, and I show up on Monday."

That's not how a 63-year-old thinks—particularly if they've never worked out or set foot in a fitness facility.

It may sound comical, but many older adults are actually waiting for you to call them and set up an appointment.

You have to tell them what to do next in every promotion. Walk them through the next steps. Make it simple.

If you want them to call and make an appointment, tell them that.

Don't do everything online either.

Boomers don't trust sharing a credit card online, especially with strangers. Anticipate that they do things differently than the under-50 crowd. They probably will want to meet you face to face before they sign even a short-term agreement.

Speaking of that, here's the third key to marketing to the mature audience.

Have a Great Introductory Offer

You've got to remember that a large portion of this population has probably never worked out—or set foot—in a gym. They're nervous, and they're not confident they'll like it … or you.

So, let them kick the tires with a trial offer … and then work really hard to get them a result they can see and feel with an experience they enjoy. If they do, our experience is they'll stay with you for a very long time.

There are no hard-and-fast, perfect plans here, and our FAI Mastermind members all vary a bit on price and duration. At Miracles, we typically offer a six-week trial offer. We know other trainers who get good results from two-week or one-month free deals.

Shelley is one of our FAI Mastermind members, and her "trial" offer is a 21-Day Transformation. She promotes the deal in the back of her fitness book which also helps her track her book's effectiveness as a marketing tool. Everyone who comes in for a visit is offered a free copy of her book with that special offer. Then, once people try her for 21 days they are hooked. Shelley typically sells the 21-Day Transformation for $89.

Beth is another one of our FAI Mastermind members. She doesn't mess around with short-term trials; she simply opens up 5–10 spots in her group training program and you have to sign on for 7 months or longer. She sells it out every time! Beth happens to be a Boomer herself … which is an added advantage for her business!

Our best advice is to offer something that's *similar* in price to your normal monthly agreement (so you don't attract bargain hunters) and long enough that you can help them achieve a measurable result for their investment.

Know your market and your numbers, then experiment to find what works for you.

Chapter 3

What's Holding You Back?

If working with Boomers is so great, why aren't more clubs doing it?

If you've never worked with mature adults, there are a few common skill hurdles to keep in mind.

Here are the big three we hear:

- Fear you'll "break" them
- Thinking you need special equipment
- Oversight—totally missing how big the opportunity is

Getting certified as an Functional Aging Specialist will help you anticipate and adapt your workouts for their most important needs. And, as you'll learn by studying functional fitness, you don't need special equipment for a good workout.

As for oversight, we hope we've helped you get past that hurdle by now.

Since this book is about getting clients, let's dig into the marketing-related issues that can hold you back and wipe those off the planet so you can launch into this market and take advantage of your competitors' fear and oversight.

Not Having the Right Credentials

After years of hype marketing, people over 50 are particularly annoyed by being sold junk and cheap alternatives. They want the best they can afford and that means they are going to do their homework on you and your credibility.

Being a certified Functional Aging Specialist gives you internationally recognized proof that you are professionally trained to take care of their unique needs.

Not Sharing Success Stories

We just covered this in depth, but let's review it again. Functional fitness is a totally new concept to most Boomers and seniors, which is why you've got to keep telling stories until they "get it."

Until you build up your own client list and testimonials, this may be a little hard to do.

We highly recommend you subscribe to our partner's magazine and social media accounts for inspiration. Marc Middleton's media business, **Growing Bolder**™ (GrowingBolder.com) specializes in telling engaging stories you can pull from and share while you build your own library of material.

If you're a licensed **Ageless Fitness**™ training facility (more information in the back of this book), you get access to custom-branded Growing Bolder materials and other done-for-you campaigns. You'll find more on that license in the back of this book.

Wrong Branding

It still kills us to see the number of personal trainers promoting oil-covered bikini and mankini body builder images to attract the 50+ market.

Nothing makes a quality, affluent client turn and run faster than feeling like they're entering a meat market.

If you want to get into this business, you've got to view your marketing and your facility with a new set of eyes. Posters, magazines, ads, images, even the smell of your facility can make or break a four-figure contract in less than five seconds.

The mature market wants facilities and trainers who specialize in them and their needs so make sure your marketing reflects their interests … not yours.

Thinking Once & Done Marketing

Attracting your ideal clients at this age is definitely a marathon, not a sprint.

The 50+ crowd is busy, and they have a lot going on all the time. It's highly likely, even probable, that your perfect advertisement may land in their hands right when they're leaving for Europe or preparing for a grandchild's arrival.

Your great offer may just have to wait on their plans. Plan your marketing around the goal of getting multiple "touches" to the same audience over time. Never give up on any idea after one try or one week.

Getting fitness clients takes steady effort. The best campaigns build on each other.

We'll show you how we do that in chapter 5. But first, we've got to discuss finding people who are ready for your message.

About FAI Mastermind:
Don't Make the Same $50,000 Mistakes We Did

When we were starting out in this business, we were in uncharted territory. No one else was selling functional fitness to mature adults and seniors, and there was no one we could lean on for proven ideas that worked in this market.

Consequently, we made a lot of mistakes and wasted a lot of time and money "winging it" until we figured out what does work.

We paid the price to learn "don't hire too much, or any staff" until opening because you never know when your opening date will actually be. Our contractor missed our opening date by 4 months! Paying staff (including a full-time manager) was a big costly mistake that took us a while to dig out from under.

We paid the price to learn other things too, like how much space and equipment we really needed. We wasted about $20,000 in rent on that mistake…and equipment too – to the tune of $10,000. The truth is, you probably need a lot less space and equipment than you think for the mature audience!

That's why we're so adamant now about supporting personal trainers, studio owners, and startups in our FAI Mastermind. Talking about, studying, and learning from "numbers" is an important part of the experience.

Our FAI Mastermind group meets in person three times a year, typically for two-day meetings.

One of the meetings is in West Lafayette, Indiana, where you'll tour our facility and learn about all aspects of our operations firsthand (including our finances and employment agreements). The other sites are typically held in conjunction with our Annual FAI Summit and then one in the West, typically San Diego, California, or Phoenix, Arizona.

In addition to these intense, in-person meet-ups, members get monthly one-on-one coaching calls and a private Facebook group so we get to share and bounce ideas off each other.

You not only get personalized support and accountability any time you need it, but you also get access to a lot of done-for-you resources, like eBooks, Facebook ads and campaigns, email templates, and more.

As we said before, we're committed to impacting one million lives by helping you profitably attract and train mature adults.

For more information on the FAI Mastermind program, visit
http://www.functionalaginginstitute.com/mastermind

Chapter 4

How to Identify Your Ideal Clients

Tried to get Boomer clients and failed? It could be due to some of the factors we discussed in the previous chapter.

Marketing to this audience is all about branding to attract their attention and then connecting with your IDEAL clients at the right time in their life.

There's a BIG difference between people who NEED your services, and people who WANT your services.

It's a pretty safe bet that every single adult over 40 has heard that they need to eat healthy foods and exercise regularly. The reality is that the vast majority willfully DON'T.

And yet, so many trainers will waste thousands of dollars trying to convince these couch potatoes that they should diet and exercise.

That's crazy. Why start at ground zero?

You'll get much faster results marketing to people already interested in making health changes.

Let's illustrate this idea with a story from our FAI Mastermind group.

One of our members was struggling to make ends meet and her marketing wasn't working. Her studio was located in a strip mall, and she noticed that the restaurant next door attracted a steady crowd of retirees for breakfast every day.

In general, she described this morning crowd as overweight and out of shape. "They're perfect because they really need this!" she'd say.

The restaurant owner (her friend) allowed her to promote her business by setting up a small display of her new book right on the cashier's counter. Because it was such a great opportunity, she even gave the books away for free.

Now, using a free book like this can be extremely effective, so, on the surface, she thought she had a good plan. But 250 free books later (which cost her about $600), she still didn't have her first lead.

"I don't understand why it's not working," she groaned.

The problem was her targeting.

Think of it like Facebook targeting. Would you want to zone in on 68-year-old, retired couples who go out on weekdays for a sausage, gravy, and biscuit breakfast?

Or, would you have better luck targeting a 68-year-old couple that shops at a farmer's market and subscribes to *Eating Well*?

It's pretty likely that the typical Monday-morning-breakfast crowd isn't thinking about making significant health changes over bacon and eggs with friends. It's just not where they are emotionally at that stage in time—at least not yet.

The good news is that all 250 of those leads probably read some of the book and still have it on their shelf or nightstand. And, many may reference it again the moment they experience some sort of "wake up call," when getting in shape becomes a priority.

In fact, that's exactly what our trainer discovered a few months later, when she got her first new member from the restaurant book offer. Since then she's discovered better placements for the book and her marketing and having great success.

But, here's the lesson we had for her in that FAI Mastermind meeting and for you today.

Whenever possible, you want to position your marketing for times and places when health and fitness is already on their mind.

You'll find your marketing dollars go much further in front of these "seekers." Here's where to find them:

Finding Effective Moments to Capture Attention

- When they're already focused on making healthy choices … such as shopping at a Whole Foods Market, farmer's market, The Vitamin Shoppe, etc.

- When they're thinking about being physically active … such as at a walk-for-the-cure event, an athletic shoe or sporting goods store, a golf course, a tennis club, or while planning a big vacation.

- When they're in the waiting room for a doctor or physical therapy appointment.

- When they're focused on self-care or their looks, such as at a dermatologist, dentist, massage therapist, hair salon, etc.

- When a friend or loved one is diagnosed with a serious health condition—or they personally experience an alarming event or scary doctor's report.

- When their friend (who happens to be your client) is celebrating a milestone or good news report that gets their attention.

The bottom line: It's easier, faster, and less expensive to convert a prospect into a hot lead and client when they're already interested in the message you have to offer.

Now, let's talk about the most effective marketing tactics to help make sure you're there in those moments.

Chapter 5

How to Get Clients FAST

We've talked about WHAT to say (and not say).

We've talked about the best WHO to say it to (seekers).

We've talked about WHEN to say it (and when it's mostly a waste of your time and money).

Now, let's get to the nitty gritty: WHERE to say it.

Online vs. Offline Marketing

Marketing to people over 50 is more effective when you mix both online and offline marketing. But with this audience, you've got to think offline a lot more than you're used to.

There are many older adults that will NEVER create a Facebook account or sign up for an email marketing list.

Yes, we said NEVER. A lot of Boomers are stubborn that way.

That doesn't mean they aren't active in their community, affluent, or well connected.

The best strategy is to reach them offline, and then follow up your efforts online.

Let's start with online strategies since that's what you are probably most familiar with, and we can cover it quickly.

Our Most Effective Online Marketing Tactics

For the purposes of this book, we'll define online as digital marketing through a screen. This world can be complex and require a lot of split testing, but in our experience, there are two primary winners:

$ – Build an Email List of Prospects

Email marketing is priceless because it allows you to stay connected and keep building a relationship until a prospect is ready to say YES to your invitation.

And don't listen to people who say email marketing is dead. The great thing about retired adults and affluent women who don't work is that they tend to read more email than the normal "working-class" age group.

Just because YOU are inundated with email and don't read all of your newsletters doesn't mean that your ideal audience won't.

A good weekly newsletter, packed with interesting stories, tips, and recipes, will get opened most of the time.

To get Boomer fitness clients fast, you need to make it your #1 priority to build an email list of good prospects as quickly as you can.

The ideas that follow will help you find these people.

Start by going through every local connection you already have and reach out to them with a single, personal email invitation. Don't SPAM people, and never put people on your bulk mailing list without their permission.

Just reach out individually to each contact and tell them you specialize in health and fitness for mature adults. Then, ask them if they'd like to be included on your mailing list AND ask if they'd like two weeks of FREE personal training with you.

Your first goal is to get at least 100 emails of interested adults. Your second goal is to fill your schedule with two-week trials so you can get clients, testimonials, and referrals.

As you build your email list, you'll want and need to stay in contact with them weekly.

That can get difficult when you consider all the other things you need to be doing, so we recommend you don't attempt to write your own content every time. For a great done-for-you email newsletter, we recommend using FitPro Newsletter™.

First of all, FitPro is a complete email marketing and contact management system, designed to help personal trainers track and sort prospects based on their interests.

Even better, FitPro is loaded with tons of done-for-you content, including a weekly email newsletter. That's the newsletter we've been using for Miracles for years, and our clients and prospects love it.

FitPro also has done-for-you landing pages, ad campaigns, free reports, social media graphics, and more. Some of it is geared to the younger market, but there's still plenty of great stuff for the 50+ crowd. Try FitPro for 30 days for just $1 by using our affiliate link at: http://functionalaginginstitute.com/fitpro.

Inside FitPro Newsletter, you'll find a lot more you can experiment with over time.

But first, for the fastest path to getting clients, start with building up your email contact list.

$ – Run Facebook Ads

When it comes to reaching Boomers, Facebook is definitely the social media channel of choice. They're there more than any other online channel.

We do know that 70% of Boomers in the US have a Facebook account, and that the majority of Boomer women are reachable through both Facebook and email strategies … so this is still definitely a marketing strategy to leverage.

Getting your daily posts into the newsfeed for free is becoming harder and harder, but the effectiveness of Facebook ads, at least at the time of this writing, is still very strong.

So for now—be prepared to spend money to get your posts in front of your ideal target demographic. (If you're new to Facebook targeting, be sure to get help and start small.)

Whether you boost a post or run an ad, your primary goal is to tell stories to attract interest and to acquire email addresses to build your email list.

Stories will get you more likes, clicks, and shares, which can make even an inexpensive boost more effective. Just don't forget to end every story with a "what to do next" (like sign up for a trial offer or join your newsletter list) or you'll waste your marketing dollars just entertaining people.

You can also use some of the done-for-you Facebook campaigns available inside FitPro to build your email list. The campaigns include short eBooks and guides that prospects download in exchange for joining your mailing list.

Once again, FitPro makes Facebook and email marketing much easier, which is why we're such a big fan of it for our trainers.

OK, to review, here is the primary focus for your online marketing:

1. Build a growing list of subscribers for your weekly email newsletter.

2. Run Facebook ads to attract new leads.

Our Most Effective Offline Marketing

As we already mentioned, you're marketing to people who've become masters at avoiding "the gym" their entire adult life. And now, you have the opportunity (and responsibility) to say something that's going to change their minds and get them moving.

Not only are you hoping to improve on your own success by doing that … but their friends, family, and loved ones are likely hoping someone will get their attention too.

To do that will often require a deeper engagement than you can get through a Facebook post.

You don't convince a 66-year-old to adopt a new lifetime habit of exercise based on an inspirational quote, morning workout video, or a holiday discount offer.

You need stories, the time to tell stories, and their full "listening" attention.

That's most effectively done offline.

Pay attention now.

What we're about to share is proven to be very effective—especially when we show you how to work these things together at once.

$ – Speak to Local Groups as Often as You Can

This one may be the hardest tactic for those of you who don't like public speaking. But, it's definitely a profitable use of your time so don't turn away just yet.

Your goal is to get as many guest-speaker opportunities as you can so you can meet your ideal clients in a situation where you're a featured authority (not a salesperson!).

Your speech doesn't have to be an elaborate presentation. You're just looking for 10–30 minute opportunities to share a few stories, teach people about functional fitness, and then invite them to take the next step.

Connecting with people face-to-face is what's most important.

Even a five-minute speech is longer than an average website visit or YouTube video view, and it is MUCH more effective!

You'll be surprised how many groups there are in your area that are looking for health-related guest speakers. Here's a list of ideas to get you going:

Civic Groups	American Diabetes Foundation
Philanthropic Groups	American Heart Association
Rotary, Kiwanis, Lions, Elks, etc.	Parkinson's and MS Support Groups
Retirees Clubs	Arthritis & Joint Replacement Support Groups

Church Groups

Men's or Women's Groups

Business Lunch-n-Learns

4H Homemakers

Quilting/Knitting Clubs

Health Education Centers

Cardiovascular Health Clinics

Rehab Centers

Home Care Organizations

Caregiver Support Groups

The easiest way to start is by asking your current clients if they're a member of any clubs or organizations that invite guest speakers. If they are, request an email introduction to the club's organizer or program director.

In my experience, these groups are often smaller than 15–20 people at a time, so it's easy connect on a personal level … and not that scary.

For most of these groups, the targeting is pretty specific as well so finding your ideal audience is pretty easy.

Just get the contact information for the program director and send them a short, friendly email offering to speak to their members about functional fitness for adults over 50 … or people with Parkinson's … or joint pain … etc.

Whenever you can, try to niche the topic just a bit for the audience, and you'll be more likely to get an invitation to speak.

If you know a member of the group, be sure to share that in your email.

$ – Join a Business Networking Group

At first, most personal trainers think that business-to-business (B2B) networking is a waste of time. That's a costly misconception.

We've been a member of a local B2B networking group for 11 years, and we've tracked over $100,000 in new clients and business directly from the group.

Networking groups offer access to three audiences at once.

First, you get access to the members themselves … most of whom are probably over 45 and good candidates for your services because they're busy business owners neglecting their own health.

Second, those business owners have employees, and you can arrange a discounted membership offer for those employees and their family members as an "employee benefit" that costs them nothing except maybe hosting a lunch-n-learn for you.

Third, of course, these business owners are well connected in the community. Once you teach them what you do and the specific referrals you're looking for, they become your marketing team.

A networking group is also a good support community to help you keep abreast of upcoming community events and small groups you may want to plug into. Things like health fairs, aging-in-place conferences, caregiver events, etc.

With rare exceptions, every community has a couple of different business-to-business networking groups. Your local Chamber of Commerce is a good start. BNI (Business Networking International) is one of the most common in the US.

If you want to grow your business fast, block the time on your calendar and get involved in a strong, networking group.

And don't forget to be a responsible active member. Networking groups work when people know you're there to support them as well. Done well, these people can become great friends in your community.

$ – Run a Direct Mail Postcard Campaign

If you think postcard mailings are dead or don't work, think again.

Rob, in Alabama, got this one idea from us when he came to one of our two-day FAI Mastermind meetings. While talking about targeting, Rob realized most of his ideal clients lived in two gated golf communities close to his studio.

So he started direct-mailing postcards to just those two neighborhoods, and it worked. Rob stopped wasting money on other marketing efforts that weren't working and just focused on his postcard campaigns.

So what's the secret to a postcard campaign?

Repetition.

You can't just send one and be done.

We teach personal trainers to send three postcards over a 30-day period. Repetition is a key part of the plan because the first one almost always goes into the recipient's trash.

It's the THIRD consecutive postcard that produces the biggest response.

Most trainers stop at one, maybe two, and then they say, "I tried that, and it didn't work."

If that's you, try again with 3 postcards spaced inside a 21- to 30-day period.

Putting together your campaign isn't that hard either.

The US Postal Service (USPS) makes it easy and affordable to do this with their Every Door Direct Mail (EDDM) offering. (Canada has a similar service called Neighbourhood Mail, and we suspect other countries do as well.)

These services allow you to pick neighborhood routes with targeting information that is almost as detailed as what is available for Facebook ads. You simply go to the USPS website and research which neighborhoods (or mail routes) are most likely to have your ideal clients based on age, household income, interests, etc.

The system tells you how many homes are on your preferred route(s), and then you work with your local printer to design and address postcards to the homes for as little as 18 cents each.

Of course, there's a bit more to the process, but it's surprisingly easy to do. And, most printers are now EDDM certified, which means they'll handle most of the details for you.

Best of all, you should be able to run the whole campaign, printing, postage, and all for about 50¢ a home per run!

Totally affordable, easily repeatable, and it works!

Just be sure to send all 3 postcards to the same route within 30 days. You can stay within a smaller budget by just doing one route at a time.

The final idea is a biggie, and, when combined with the earlier ideas, makes everything much more effective.

$ – Have Your Own Book

Did you notice that we didn't say you had to WRITE your own book? We'll get to that in a minute! First, let's discuss why HAVING your own book—with your name as author—is one of the most effective marketing decisions you'll ever make.

- Being a published fitness author makes you stand out as an EXPERT.
- Boomers want to work with experts.
- Boomers actually read books.
- Boomers research before they buy.
- People feel comfortable giving their friends your book as an easy referral.
- Books let you tell a lot of stories.
- Books don't feel salesy.
- Books don't get thrown in the trash like business cards or fliers.

Let us share a story to illustrate this point.

One of our clients is a remarkable success story in her 80s. Every time she goes to see her doctor, he tells her, "Whatever you're doing, keep doing it!" Of course, he knows she trains at our studio and he's become a supporter of our functional fitness program.

One day we asked her if she'd take her doctor a handful of our books and ask if he would be willing to put them in his waiting area. Her doctor read the book, and now he's sharing it with his patients. Our client even takes a new stack to every checkup for us!

This relationship has been going on for about a year when another patient of his called us for an appointment. He came walking in with the copy of the book his doctor had given him.

Embarrassed, he admitted that the doctor had given him the book and the suggestion to join about a year ago. He'd held on to it until he was finally ready to take the advice.

Because he'd gotten our book from his doctor, and he'd read several of our success stories, there wasn't any need for us to "sell" him on anything.

That day, he signed up for our most expensive private client package and paid in full for a year's worth of training.

That ONE book resulted in a $6,000+ annual contract! Statistically, at Miracles, he'll probably spend $20,000 to $50,000 with us in the next few years!

All from one book that cost us $2.50!

A book has remarkable longevity. It's waiting to tell your story when the person is ready to listen.

That's not something a business card or flier can do for you.

People are also much more likely to give a friend (or patient) your book than a business card or flier. It makes them feel good to give someone a real gift with inherent retail value.

Trainers who have a book intentionally crafted to attract their ideal clients—and inspire them to action—discover it's a game changer for their business.

FAI Mastermind member Lisa (Corpus Christi, Texas) tracked $57,000 in new client business from the first year she had her book.

At the same time, Shelley used her book to launch her brand new fitness center in Saskatoon, Saskatchewan in Canada. She kept records and tracked $103,000 in new client contracts from her book in 14 months! Here's a picture of Shelley's book featuring her and her high-profile client, a local news anchor! (Shelley's star client earned her book instant recognition!)

Having a book makes all your other marketing efforts more effective.

- It's easier to get speaking engagements when you're a published author.

- It's easier to get attention on social media when people are talking about you and your book.

- It's easier to get your clients to refer you by giving friends your book.

- It's easier to get people to subscribe to your newsletter list with a book as your free giveaway.

- It's faster and easier to close a sale when a prospect has read your book.

And let's face it…

It's quite satisfying to know you're viewed as more of an expert than your competitors because you're a published fitness author.

Here's the really good news: **you don't even need to write your book yourself!**

We've already written all the content you need to publish your own fitness book in as fast as 30 days. We'll tell you how to do that in chapter 7.

For now, just imagine how being a published expert on fitness for mature adults could help you stand out and get a lot more attention for your business … FAST!

Chapter 6

Selling Boomers on Fitness

We're going to shift gears and talk about sales.

We're going to take you through our sales process. Specifically how we sell fitness programs to people and how we get them to realize they need to buy three sessions per week of personal training.

At Miracles, we offer both one-on-one private training and small group training. In the sales meeting, we're not really attached to one or the other because we have the trainers to handle both.

Our primary goal is to encourage them to commit to 3 sessions a week because we know at that pace we'll quickly get them great results.

If they happen to only choose twice a week, we're still going to get them pretty good results. Those are really the only options they have with us—private or group sessions, and two times or three times a week.

We begin by going through their health history. We talk about their balance issues, joint issues, joint replacements, muscular and skeletal issues. They know all of these things are starting to slip a little bit. They often think they need some strength training and some cardio, like walking on a treadmill. While walking is important, it's certainly not going to get us maximum physical function.

This chart helps them see why we use the functional aging training model to hit all the components of human function so they can move better—not just walk.

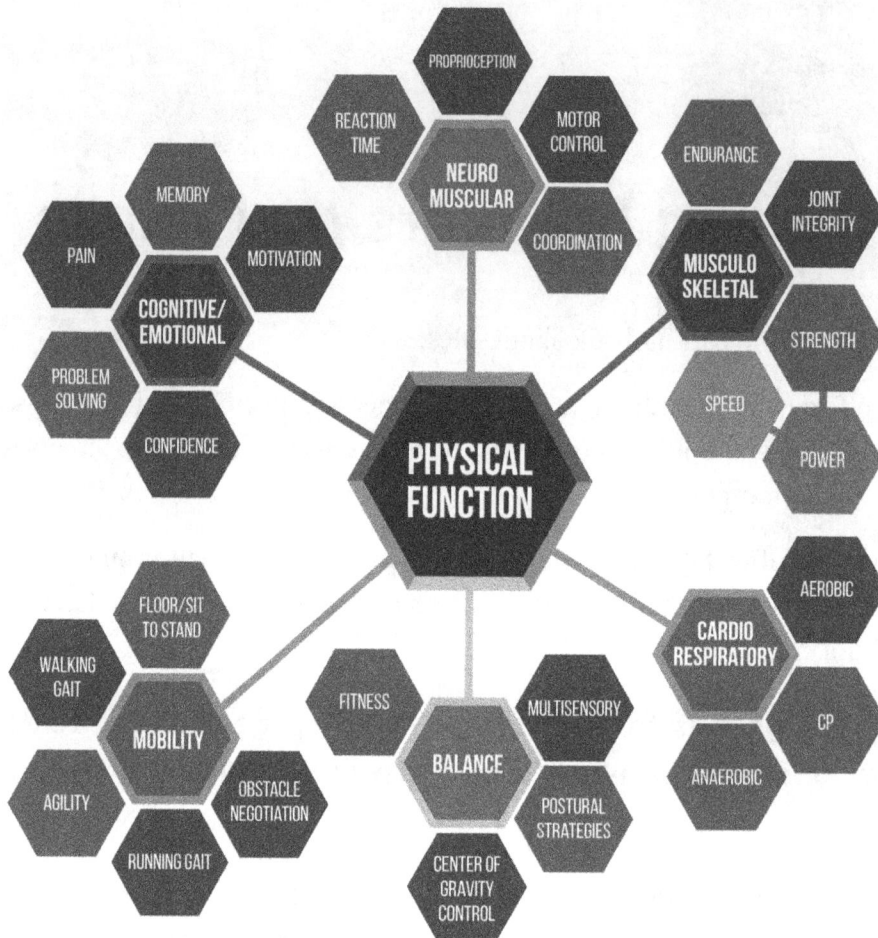

The 6 Areas of Physical Function, Functional Aging Institute

This reiterates why our credentials are important. You're a trained Functional Aging Specialist (FAS)—or at least you should be.

We tell our trainers to use as much of their experience with us and other professionals in this field as possible. Use the fact that you're certified, that you've attend FAI events and webinars, that you've heard our experts speak, etc.

You're probably an expert in your community at a level that most trainers are not. You have to leverage that.

If they're sitting in front of you to buy a fitness program, they already assume you have some level of expertise. So share that. Show that. Demonstrate that.

If you're not a certified Functional Aging Specialist, you need to get that done quickly. You absolutely need to have that credential. As we mentioned, your prospect is looking for the best. Someone they can trust that won't hurt them.

We also want you to be an FAS so we can find you. Prospects are contacting us every week asking for a functional aging specialist in their community.

"Where's a functional aging specialist in Boca Raton? Where's a functional aging specialist in Albuquerque?" You name the place. They find our website and look on the map for an FAS in their area. You're not on the map if you're not certified. You've got to get on the map.

You're not selling a fitness program. You're selling human function.

We talk a lot about how often trainers make the mistake of marketing fitness and selling fitness.

The reality is that the older clients get, the less interested they are in fitness and the more interested they are in living ... really living!

You are selling what fitness can do for them. You are not selling fitness. So when we sit down with a prospect, we have to hear their interests, their goals, their dreams, etc. These are what we call their NLW's: Needs, Likes, and Wants.

If we can figure out what they really like to do and want to do, the job of selling training just got way, way easier. This means you first have to listen, ask questions, conduct a thorough interview, and only then present a solution that meets their needs, likes, and wants.

With this approach, you really aren't selling a fitness program at all. You are helping them choose what program is going to serve their life goals the best.

You become their buying consultant, instead of someone selling them a fitness routine.

Sell the Blue Line

At this point in the conversation, we draw this chart and sell them "the blue line."

Functional Trajectory of Aging

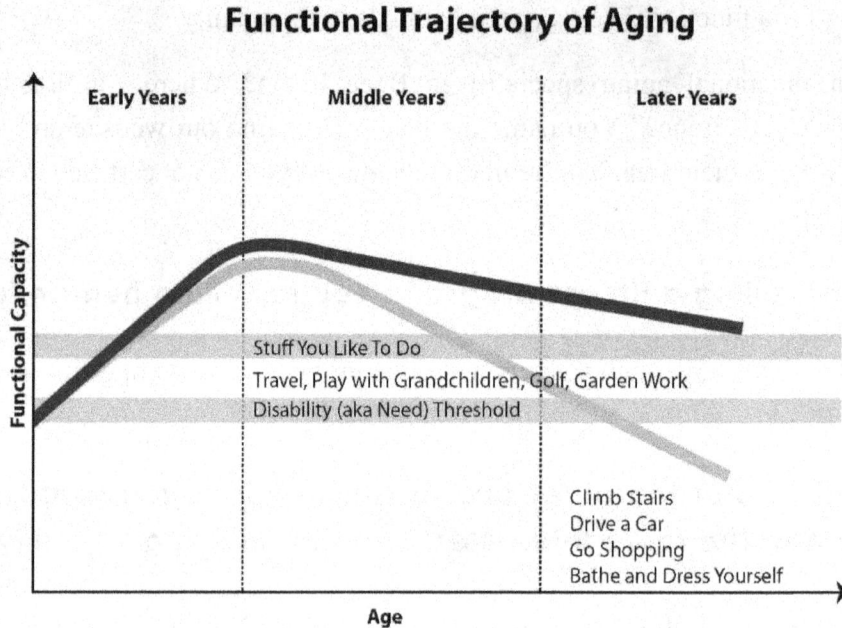

©Functional Aging Institute 2016

You are selling them on the concept of living well to their final days, as opposed to the traditional model of aging, which is to decline to the point of disability, sickness, frailty, and dependence.

You are ultimately presenting two very stark options: the blue line (top arc)—a line of independence, functional ability, and adventure; or the orange line (lower arc)—a line of impending decline.

Tough choice, right?

We are not selling fitness. We are selling functional longevity, independence, and the ability to continue to do all the things they enjoy in life.

Once they are ready to buy, keep it simple!

Do not overcomplicate things with multiple package options and à la carte menu choices. Offer two- or three-times-per-week training. Get them to commit, ideally to three times, and you are done!

Then offer them a short-term or long-term option.

We use 7 or 11 months. We won't explain in this book the psychology of why offering two time options works, but it does! You can use 6 and 12, or 9 and 18, but have a short- and long-term option. The long-term option should have a slight discount to incentivize the long-term commitment.

DO NOT discount paid-in-full memberships! There is simply no reason to discount when they want to pay in full. We have actually joked that we should discount the payment plan option just to get more people on regular recurring payments!

Offer an automatic payment option on a credit card or a paid-in-full option, and get them signed up and scheduled to train immediately—the same day, if possible, or the next day at the latest.

Make sure you manage your onboarding system really well!

They don't know what to wear, when to show up for their appointment, how to warm up, what to eat beforehand—assume they don't know anything. We address all those types of questions in chapter 8 of our done-for-you book. If you don't have a book yet, print out the material on a piece of paper they can take with them.

It is never good to sell someone a $3,000 training program, have them pay in full, and then have them walk out with no idea what they are supposed to do next.

Give them a checklist or show them where to find the information in your book. Then, introduce them to their trainer, give them a tour of your studio, and answer any final questions before they go.

Be sure to introduce them to people as they go, too. Many of your clients will enjoy the social aspect and the new friendships as much as anything else. That's priceless to your business.

Hold their hands for quite a while. Teach them what you expect and what you plan to do with them. Lead them well, take good care of them, and they will be loyal clients for years!

Chapter 7

How to Implement Ideas FAST!

By now, you may be feeling a bit of overwhelmed by these ideas and how you'll get them implemented.

Most trainers come to us doing WAY TOO MUCH stuff that they shouldn't be doing which is keeping them from their real income potential.

If you're still doing all the training yourself, plus the bill paying, plus the cleaning and the laundry, plus posting to Facebook, etc. … you're going to remain stuck in an awful version of an entrepreneurial Groundhog Day repeating the same events over and over and over.

You've got to get out from under the day-to-day operations, establish yourself as a true BUSINESS OWNER, and focus on what's most important: bringing in clients.

One of the greatest values of participating in FAI Mastermind is that you get to spend time with people who've overcome this scarcity mindset and are growing a scalable business and making more money a lot faster than before.

That experience is life changing. You learn to see the opportunities around you differently.

Building your business becomes something you really enjoy because you're getting more done and seeing results.

For more information on joining FAI Mastermind, including our next live event dates and location, visit: www.functionalaginginstitute.com/mastermind

Free Up Your Time

The first thing you need to do is free up some time … FAST!

Grab a pen and paper right now and start writing down all the repetitive tasks you're doing and figure out which ones you could stop or delegate to someone else.

Hire a college student to do laundry and clean equipment. If you've got trainers who work for you, give them additional responsibilities between sessions, etc.

Perhaps one of your first clients would like to work for you to earn a discount … or keep the bargain monthly rate they've had for way too long.

We've got FAI Mastermind members who've traded workout time for training, graphic design, cleaning, bookkeeping, even marketing.

When we first started training clients, we did everything. Then Cody moved to Arkansas to serve as an Associate Professor and Director of Clinical Studies at Harding College, which left Dan in charge of the business' day-to-day operations.

At this point, we made it a priority to hire our first trainer so Dan could get out into the community and get clients. We scaled up from there so that now Dan is able to manage Miracles and five other profitable business ventures—including the Functional Aging Institute!

It starts with thinking differently.

Back to you and your time.

Look at your training schedule. Can you condense your schedule or rearrange it to give you one business development day a week?

Can you combine several private clients into a small group? Moving just four to five individual clients to a group program could free up anywhere from three to five hours of your time A WEEK!

They get a discount and some new accountability buddies and you get some time to work on bringing in more group clients.

Yes, it's scary. Yes, it's necessary. Do it anyway.

Start thinking out of the box and get your time back FAST.

Time is money.

Think Return on Investment

When you're investing your marketing dollar, think of a slot machine or an ATM. Would you put $1 in if you knew it would give you $10 out?

Marketing works like that. You invest money in the places that are proven effective and your investment comes back in the form of client contracts that pay you much more in return!

For example, would you invest $300 in a one-year BNI membership for the opportunity to get 10 good referrals worth $200 per month each?

Or, would a $500 investment in printing and postage for a 3-time postcard campaign be worth it if it yields you three new annual memberships, totaling over $7,000?

Or the book, remember the book deal?

Lisa invested $5,700 in the production of her book and 1,300 copies that she gave away for FREE in the first several months. That investment probably felt scary at the time, but now that she's acquired over $57,000 in new clients from that decision it was a really great return on her investment!

> *We handed out just over 700 copies of our FAI books in our first 14 months and the results have been empowering! We've added over $57,000 in new memberships tracked directly to the book. That's a great return on our investment in a very short time. One of the smartest marketing decisions I've made for my business.*
>
> *– Lisa Wright, FAS*

The point is, you spend money to make money. Invest wisely in ideas that others, like us, have already proven to work.

There's no need to experiment here or to start from scratch. We've already shared, in depth, what's working for us and our trainers.

Now, we want to help you implement those ideas FASTER.

Take Advantage of Our Done-for-You Marketing

One of the biggest advantages we offer our certified Functional Aging Specialists and FAI Mastermind members is access to done-for-you marketing materials.

Having access to this caliber of professionally written marketing materials is a MAJOR competitive advantage.

We already gave you our five most effective marketing decisions in chapter 5. Now, let's recap which ones are available as done-for-you because these things are sitting out there RIGHT NOW for you to put to work in the next month or two.

☑ Done-for-You Newsletters, Ads, and Emails

With your FitPro subscription, you get a ton of done-for-you content, including a weekly newsletter, Facebook campaigns, autoresponder emails, and more.

You could hang a Do Not Disturb sign on your office door and have your newsletter branded and scheduled for delivery every week this year, a Facebook ad campaign running, and a welcome email campaign—DONE IN ONE DAY.

To enroll in a $1 trial offer, go here: FunctionalAgingInstitute.com/FitPro

DONE-FOR-YOU BOOKS

"Our #1 Strategy for Converting Leads into Clients"

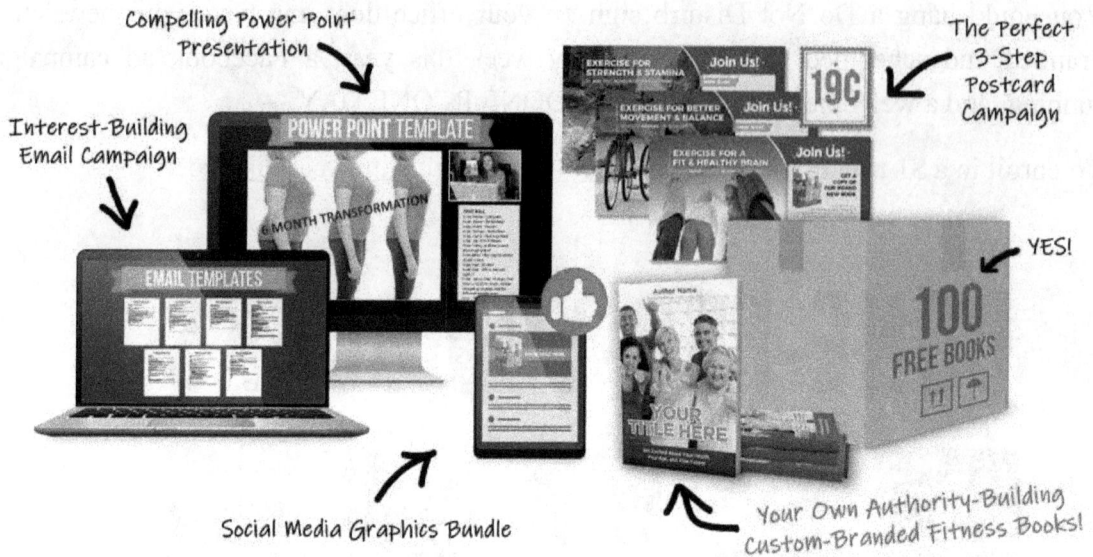

Compelling Power Point Presentation

Interest-Building Email Campaign

POWER POINT TEMPLATE

6 MONTH TRANSFORMATION

EMAIL TEMPLATES

The Perfect 3-Step Postcard Campaign

EXERCISE FOR STRENGTH & STAMINA — Join Us!

EXERCISE FOR BETTER MOVEMENT & BALANCE — Join Us!

EXERCISE FOR A FIT & HEALTHY BRAIN — Join Us!

YES!

100 FREE BOOKS

YOUR TITLE HERE — Author Name

Social Media Graphics Bundle

Your Own Authority-Building Custom-Branded Fitness Books!

☑ Done-for-You Fitness Book Bundle

Our done-for-you fitness book bundle is, by far, our single greatest done-for-you opportunity because it's so effective at getting people's attention and converting leads into clients.

Adopting a done-for-you book works a lot like using the done-for-you newsletters or emails.

We've prewritten nine chapters of content designed to convert prospects into clients. Your license allows you to customize that content, add your own title, images, branding, etc., to make it your own and use it in your local marketing.

Currently there are four content choices: *Functional Fitness, Complete Fitness,* and *Body Transformation.*

- **The Functional Fitness** book is written to inspire the mature adult who has probably never worked out with a personal trainer. The content helps them redefine aging and discover how functional fitness can help them live an active lifestyle for years to come.

- **The Complete Fitness** book focuses on the 6 Areas of Physical Functions diagram and stresses the importance of working with an expert to create a well-balanced fitness routine. It's written to help physically active people (typically pre-retirees) understand the value of adding cognitive, balance, and mobility elements to their existing strength & cardio routines.

- **The Body Transformation** book is written to target women age 35–55 who want to transform their health and body, but it's appropriate for all audiences. The content helps you demonstrate your expertise by debunking common fitness and weight loss myths that are wasting your ideal clients' time and money.

- **The Healthy Mindset** book is written to target frustrated adults who have "been there done that" with diets and fitness programs and had no success. The content emphasizes the value of a caring coach, group support, and regular accountability to achieve lasting health goals.

Any of the 4 books can be published with a custom-branded book jacket featuring your photos, your personal story, client testimonials, before/after images, and business branding … IN AS FAST AS 30 DAYS!

That means you could be handing out YOUR book to prospects and placing it doctors', chiropractors', dentists', and physical therapists' lobbies NEXT MONTH.

The bundle also includes done-for-you launch emails, a community presentation, postcard mailers, social media graphics, and a step-by-step marketing guidebook.

To see if a license is still available for your community, and to preview a copy of each book, visit our publishing partner's website: coauthorbooks.com/FAI

☑ Done-for-You Postcards

There's no doubt the 3-time postcard campaign works, but it's particularly effective when coupled with a book promotion, which is why we share three done-for-you postcard templates with all of our licensed books.

These postcards feature two compelling offers on each card. On one side we promote a trial membership offer. That instant deal works well for the person who's ready to get started immediately. On the other side of the card, we invite interested prospects to call or stop by to get a free copy of our book.

It's the book offer that makes the postcards really stand out

Having a picture of your book on the postcard with the words FREE grabs people's attention. (How many local trainers do you know that have a book … and are giving it away for FREE!?!)

The done-for-you postcards feature three designs as well as instructions to find a printer who can easily add your business logo and branding, then print/ship them directly for you.

It's a done-for-you project that you could easily implement in a couple of hours.

These postcards are an exclusive bonus for our licensed book authors through our publishing partner, Niche Pressworks.

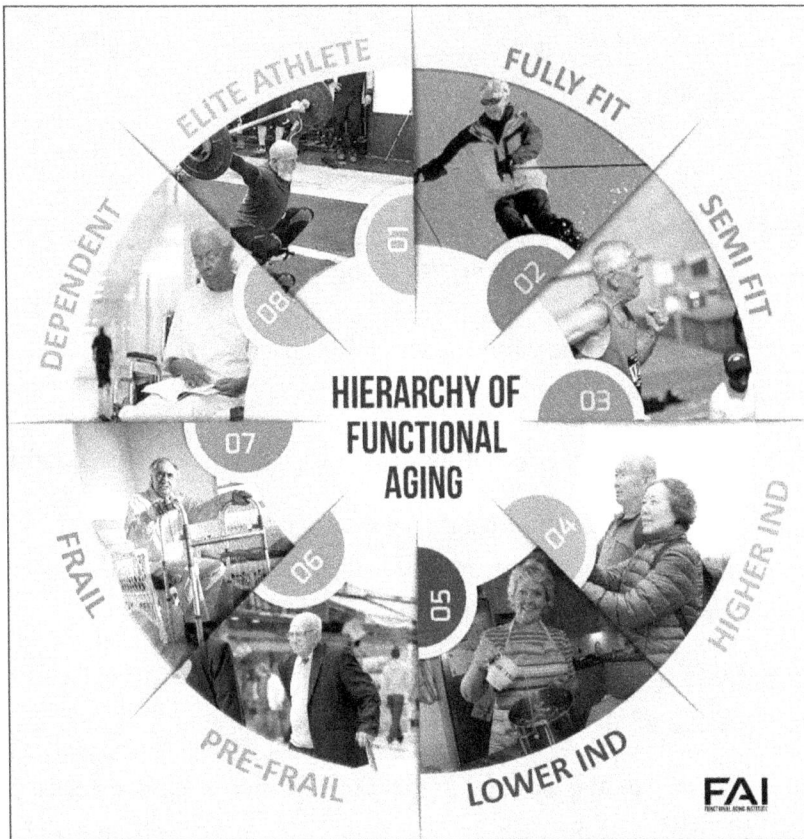

☑ Done-for-You Presentations & Images

Our final popular done-for-you marketing asset is our functional fitness slide presentations and graphic images.

We've tested and tweaked these slides and images to help you easily tell a compelling story about the new model of aging. You can grab two or three of your favorite slides for a short five-minute presentation, use them all to fill a 45-minute time slot, or pull images and graphics from the folder to use in your emails and on social media.

The slides, speaker notes, and images are available inside the members portal for our FAI Mastermind members and Ageless Fitness™ licensees.

Chapter 8

What Impact Will You Have?

Let's close by talking about what your clients can really do late in life. A lot of times, we actually write people off once they are over the age of 60, 65, or 70.

We think, "They're done with life. What more will they really try to accomplish?"

Well, we want to share a story with you that we've shared with many of our clients over the years to inspire them to think differently. Even if you are in your 30s or 40s right now, we hope it impacts your thinking about age and fitness.

A well-known individual had 27 of his most productive years taken from him. He was imprisoned for from age 45 to 72.

He wasn't put in prison in the United States, so he didn't have fitness equipment or "recreational time" like they do here in the States. In fact, the conditions were pretty poor. But, during those 27 years, he exercised faithfully. He did push-ups, sit-ups, and ran in place. He even ran laps in his cell—much to the annoyance of his cellmates.

This individual was finally released from prison at the age of 72. When he came out, he wasn't like we would expect of a prisoner after all that time. He wasn't weak, broken, frail, or old.

This man was Nelson Mandela. Three years later he would be elected president of South Africa at the age of 75.

Think Differently

Which 50-, 60-, or 70-something person in your community could you train who may have a major life accomplishment yet to come?

Maybe they are not going to become president of South Africa and change the world that dramatically. Maybe they are going to impact the generations behind them—their children, grandchildren, or great-grandchildren.

The moral of the story is that exercise in your 40s, 50s, 60s, and 70s defines what you can do later in life and how big an impact you can have.

The reason we train clients over 50 is because we believe every life has purpose and that even in your 70s, 80s, and 90s, you can still make important contributions to society.

We wish you the best in your journey to change the lives of the people in your community and join us in our efforts to positively impact one million lives around the world.

If you would like to find out more about how you can train clients in this age range, check out our programs at FunctionalAgingInstitute.com

GET CERTIFIED TODAY

FAI
FUNCTIONAL AGING INSTITUTE

BECOME A FUNCTIONAL AGING SPECIALIST

Get Your FREE FAI Starter Kit

Become a More Effective and Confident Professional

- **Become an Expert**
- **Increase Your Bottom Line**
- **Learn How to Properly Assess the Functional Abilities of Older Clients**

Get Started Here: FunctionalAgingInstitute.com

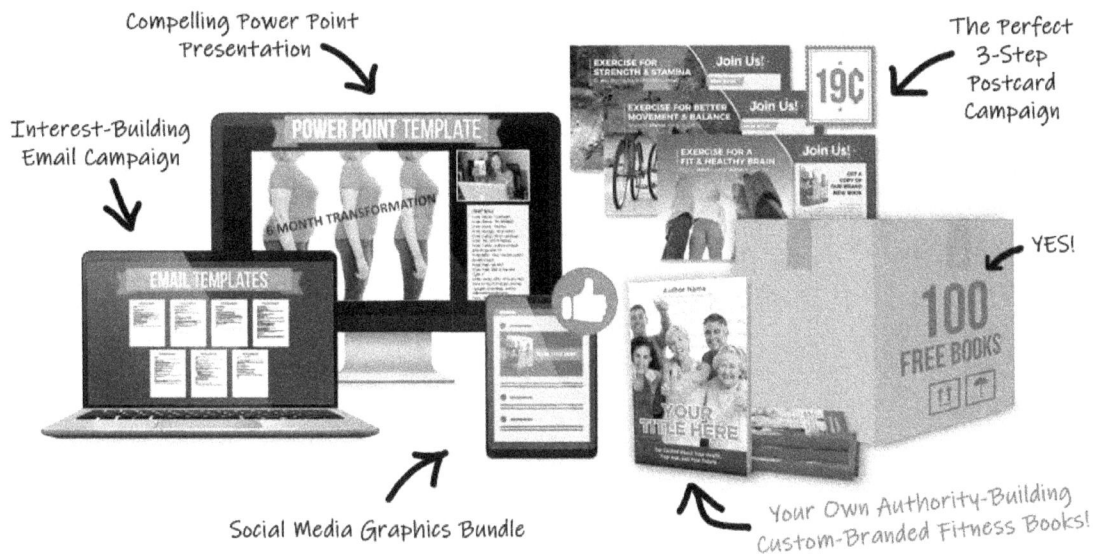

Compelling Power Point Presentation

Interest-Building Email Campaign

The Perfect 3-Step Postcard Campaign

YES!

Social Media Graphics Bundle

Your Own Authority-Building Custom-Branded Fitness Books!

Everything You Need to Position Yourself as Your Community's #1 FITNESS PRO in ONE Done-for-You Book Bundle

Make no mistake: Unless and until you're willing to do work your competitors aren't, you'll always be competing. Books are the fast path out of look-alike branding and a smart, game-changing decision.

Working with Niche Pressworks, you can get the ultimate marketing bundle including a done-for-you book published in as little as 30 days—or get coached to write your own book in three to four months.

Either way, **you could be handing out the perfect "big business card" and clearly establishing yourself as a published authority in your niche in a matter of weeks!**

Sound good to you? Remember how Lisa added $57K in new clients as a direct result of her book?

Visit the site below to get going on yours.

coauthorbooks.com/FAI

AGELESS FIT⋈ESS

Add On a Small Group Training Program for Boomers and Seniors Inside Your Gym Location and ...
INCREASE YOUR MONTHLY INCOME
BY AN AVERAGE OF $12,000

Or, Launch a Brand New Fitness Studio of Your Own!

With Ageless Fitness, you can install the equivalent of a high-end, small-group personal training studio into your gym location with no extra overhead or buildout.

Are You Up for the Challenge?
FunctionalAgingInstitute.com/AgelessFitness

Meet FAI's Co-Founders

Cody Sipe, PhD

Cody Sipe has an extensive background in the fitness industry with 20 years of experience as a personal trainer, fitness instructor, program director, exercise physiologist, and club owner. He is currently an Associate Professor and Director of Clinical Research in the physical therapy program at Harding University.

He has spent his career researching, developing, and practicing the most effective training strategies to improve function in older adults. He has completed certifications as an ACSM Exercise Specialist, ACSM

Registered Clinical Exercise Physiologist, FallProof Balance and Mobility Enhancement Specialist, and more. His secondary area of expertise is in the prevention and management of chronic disease conditions, especially those that accompany the aging process, such as arthritis, cardiovascular disease, diabetes, and osteoporosis. In 2005, he was honored with the IDEA Program Director of the Year award.

Dan Ritchie, PhD

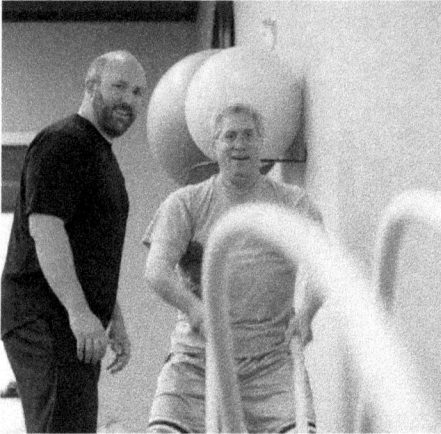

Dan Ritchie has a broad background in the fitness industry, including training and management in commercial, for-profit, not-for-profit, and educational facilities. He has expertise in personal training for special populations: athletes, stroke recovery, Parkinson's, multiple sclerosis, cerebral palsy, Fibromyalgia, Alzheimer's, etc.

He has also worked on state-funded research on exercise for patients with severe dementia Alzheimer's type.

In 2014, *PFP Magazine* named him Personal Trainer of the Year. He regularly presents at national and regional conferences and has been active on committees for the American College of Sports Medicine.

www.ingramcontent.com/pod-product-compliance
Lightning Source LLC
Chambersburg PA
CBHW051232200326
41519CB00025B/7344